Oracle SQL*Plus
Pocket Reference

Jonathan Gennick

O'REILLY®

Beijing • Cambridge • Farnham • Köln • Paris • Sebastopol • Taipei • Tokyo

Oracle SQL*Plus Pocket Reference

by Jonathan Gennick

Copyright © 2000 O'Reilly & Associates, Inc. All rights reserved.
Printed in the United States of America.

Published by O'Reilly & Associates, Inc., 101 Morris Street,
Sebastopol, CA 95472.

Editor: Deborah Russell

Production Editor: Jeffrey Holcomb

Cover Design: Ellie Volckhausen and Edie Freedman

Printing History:

April 2000:   First Edition.

1-56592-941-1   [7/00]
[C]

Table of Contents

Oracle SQL*Plus Pocket Reference

Introduction

The *Oracle SQL*Plus Pocket Reference* is a quick-reference guide to SQL*Plus. Most of this book consists of a SQL*Plus syntax reference. While I don't intend this book to be used as a tutorial for learning SQL*Plus, you will also find sections that quickly review the basics of selecting data from a database and formatting that data into a report. I've also included a chapter on SQL statement tuning showing you how to use Oracle's EXPLAIN PLAN statement and describing all the optimizer hints.

The purpose of this pocket reference is to help SQL*Plus users find the syntax of specific language elements. It is not a self-contained user guide; basic knowledge of SQL*Plus is assumed. For more information, see *Oracle SQL*Plus: The Definitive Guide*, by Jonathan Gennick (O'Reilly & Associates, 1999).

Acknowledgments

Thanks to Debby Russell for her tireless editing. Thanks to Ken Jacobs and Alison Holloway of Oracle Corporation for pointing me to information on the new HTML features in release 8.1.6. Thanks also to Mike Sierra who did the text conversion, and Jeff Holcomb for the copyedit and for managing the production process.

Conventions

UPPERCASE
> Indicates SQL*Plus, SQL, or PL/SQL keywords.

lowercase
> Indicates user-defined items such as table names.

Italic
> Indicates filenames, emphasis, introduction of new terms, and parameter names.

Constant width
> Used for code examples.

[ ] Used in syntax descriptions to denote optional elements.

{ } Used in syntax descriptions to denote a required choice.

| Used in syntax descriptions to separate choices.

__ Used in syntax descriptions to indicate that the underlined option is the default.

Interacting with SQL*Plus

This section covers essential information that you need to know in order to interact with SQL*Plus. Here you will learn how to start SQL*Plus, enter commands, delimit strings, and name variables.

Starting SQL*Plus

SQL*Plus is almost always invoked by issuing the *sqlplus* command from your operating system command prompt. On Microsoft Windows systems, you also have the option of selecting an icon from the Start menu. Early releases of SQL*Plus on Windows used executable names such as PLUS33 and PLUS80W depending on the specific release number and on whether the DOS version or the Windows version was to be invoked.

Syntax for the sqlplus command

The syntax used to invoke SQL*Plus looks like this:

```
sqlplus [[-S[ILENT]] [-R[ESTRICT] level]
   [-M[ARKUP] markup_options]
   [username[/password][@connect]|/|/NOLOG]
   [@scriptfile [arg1 arg2 arg3...]]] | - | -?
```

The -RESTRICT and -MARKUP parameters are new in release 8.1.6. The descriptions of the parameters follow:

-S[ILENT]

Tells SQL*Plus to run in silent mode. No startup messages will be displayed; no command prompt will be displayed; no commands will be echoed to the screen.

-R[ESTRICT] *level*

Restricts what the user can do from SQL*Plus. The *level* must be one of the following:

1 Disables the EDIT, HOST, and ! commands.

2 Disables the EDIT, HOST, !, SAVE, SPOOL, and STORE commands.

3 Disables the EDIT, GET, HOST, !, SAVE, START, @, @@, SPOOL, and STORE commands.

Level 3 also disables the reading of the *login.sql* file. The *glogin.sql* file will be read, but restricted commands won't be executed.

-M[ARKUP] *markup_options*

Allows you to specify the markup language to use when generating output. Except for HTML, all markup options are optional. The following are valid markup options:

HTML [ON | OFF]

Specifies the markup language to use and enables or disables the use of that markup language. In release 8.1.6, this is a mandatory option.

HEAD *text*

Specifies content for the <head> tag. The tag ends up being written as <head *text*>.

BODY *text*
> Specifies content for the <body> tag. The tag ends up being written as <body *text*>.

ENTMAP {ON | OFF}
> Controls whether SQL*Plus uses HTML equivalents such as &lt and &gt for special characters.

SPOOL {ON | OFF}
> Controls whether SQL*Plus writes to the spool file using plain text or the specified markup language (currently HTML).

PRE[FORMAT] {ON | OFF}
> Controls whether spooled report output is enclosed within <pre> … </pre> tags.

> On some operating systems, you need to enclose the entire string of markup options within double quotes.

username[*/password*][*@connect*]
> Is your database login information.

/ Connects you to a local database using operating-system authentication.

/NOLOG
> Tells SQL*Plus to start without connecting to a database first.

scriptfile
> Is the name of a SQL*Plus script file. SQL*Plus will start up, execute the file, and then exit.

arg1 agr2 arg3
> Are optional command-line arguments to pass to your script. Separate arguments by at least one space.

- Causes SQL*Plus to display a short summary of this syntax.

-? Causes SQL*Plus to display version and copyright information.

Entering Commands

How you enter commands in SQL*Plus depends a bit on whether you are entering a command to SQL*Plus itself or are entering a SQL statement or a PL/SQL block.

Entering SQL*Plus commands

Commands such as DESCRIBE, COLUMN, TTITLE, SET, and all the others listed in the "SQL*Plus Command Reference" section are commands to SQL*Plus itself. These must be entered on one line and are executed immediately after you enter them. For example:

```
SET ECHO ON
DESCRIBE employee
```

SQL*Plus commands may optionally be terminated by a semicolon. For example:

```
PROMPT This semicolon won't print.;
CONNECT system/manager;
```

You can change this behavior of SQL*Plus towards semicolons by changing the SQLTERMINATOR setting.

Long SQL*Plus commands may be continued onto multiple physical lines. The SQL*Plus continuation character is a hyphen (-). Use it at the end of a physical line to continue a long SQL*Plus command to the next line. The following three lines, for example, are treated as one by SQL*Plus:

```
COLUMN employee_id -
FORMAT 099999 -
HEADING 'Emp ID'
```

The space in front of the continuation character is optional. Quote strings may also be continued. For example:

```
SELECT 'Hello-
World!' FROM dual;
```

When you are continuing a quoted string, any spaces before the continuation character will be included in the string. The line break also counts as one space.

Entering SQL statements

SQL statements may span multiple lines and must always be terminated. This may be done using either a semicolon (;) or a forward slash (/). For example:

```
SELECT user
FROM dual;
SELECT user
FROM dual
/
```

In both of these cases, the SQL statement will be entered into a buffer known as the *SQL buffer* and then will be executed. You may also terminate a SQL statement using either a blank line or a period, in which case the statement is stored in the buffer but not executed. For example:

```
SQL> SELECT user
  2  FROM dual
  3
SQL> SELECT user
  2  FROM dual
  3  .
```

Use the SET SQLTERMINATOR command to change the terminator from a semicolon to some other character. Use SET SQLBLANKLINES ON to allow blank lines within a SQL statement. To execute the statement currently in the buffer, enter a forward slash on a line by itself.

Entering PL/SQL blocks

PL/SQL blocks may span multiple lines and may contain blank lines. They must be terminated by either a forward slash or a period (.) on a line by itself. For example:

```
BEGIN
    DBMS_OUTPUT.PUT_LINE('Hello World!');
END;
/

BEGIN
```

```
      DBMS_OUTPUT.PUT_LINE('Hello World!');
   END;
   .
```

When a forward slash is used, the block is sent to the server and executed immediately. When a period is used, the block is only stored in the SQL buffer. Use the SET BLOCK-TERMINATOR command to change the block terminator from a period to some other character.

Strings in SQL*Plus Commands

Many SQL*Plus-specific commands take string values as parameters. Simple strings containing no spaces or punctuation characters may be entered without quotes. Here's an example:

```
   COLUMN employee_id HEADING emp_id
```

Generally, it's safer to use quoted strings. Either single or double quotes may be used. For example:

```
   COLUMN employee_id HEADING 'Emp #'
   COLUMN employee_id HEADING "Emp #"
```

To embed quotes in a string, either double them or use a different enclosing quote. The following two commands have equivalent results:

```
   COLUMN employee_id HEADING '''Emp #'''
   COLUMN employee_id HEADING "'Emp #'"
```

The single exception to these rules is the PROMPT command. All quotes used in a PROMPT command will appear in the output.

Specifying Filenames

Several SQL*Plus commands allow you to specify a filename. In all cases, you may also include a path and/or an extension with the name. For example:

```
   SPOOL my_report
   SPOOL c:\temp\my_report
   SPOOL create_synonyms.sql
```

Most file-related commands assume a default extension if you don't supply one. The default varies by command.

Naming Variables

SQL*Plus allows you to declare two types of variables: user variables and bind variables. The rules for naming each type are different.

User variable names may contain letters, digits, and underscores (_) in any order. They are case-insensitive and are limited to 30 characters in length.

Bind variable names must begin with a letter, but after that may contain letters, digits, underscores, dollar signs ($), and number signs (#). They also are case-insensitive and are limited to 30 characters in length.

Using column aliases

If a SELECT statement includes columns that are expressions, Oracle will generate a column name based on the expression. Take a look at the following SQL statement:

```
SELECT SUM(hours_logged)
FROM project_hours
WHERE project_id = 1001;
```

The name of the column returned by this query will be SUM(HOURS_LOGGED). That means that any COLUMN commands used to format the output will need to look like this:

```
COLUMN SUM(HOURS_LOGGED) -
HEADING 'Total Hours'
```

As your expressions become more complicated, the Oracle-generated names become difficult to deal with. It's better to use a column alias to supply a more user-friendly name for the computed column. For example:

```
SELECT SUM(hours_logged) total_hours
FROM project_hours
WHERE project_id = 1001;
```

Now the column name is obvious. It's total_hours, and it won't change even if the expression changes.

Selecting Data

The SELECT statement is the key to getting data out of an Oracle database. It's also very likely the most commonly executed SQL statement from SQL*Plus.

The SELECT Statement

The basic form of the SELECT statement looks like this:

```
SELECT column_list
FROM table_list
WHERE conditions
GROUP BY column_list
HAVING conditions
ORDER BY column_list;
```

The lists in this syntax are comma-delimited. The column list, for example, is a comma-delimited list of column names or expressions identifying the data that you want the query to return.

Selecting columns from a table

To retrieve columns from a table, list the columns you want following the SELECT keyword, place the table name after the FROM keyword, and execute your statement. The following query returns a list of tables that you own together with the names of their assigned tablespaces:

```
SELECT table_name, tablespace_name
    FROM user_tables;
```

Ordering query results

You can use the ORDER BY clause to sort the results of a query. The following example sorts the results by table name:

```
SELECT table_name, tablespace_name
FROM user_tables
ORDER BY table_name;
```

The default is to sort in ascending order. You can specify descending order using the DESC keyword. For example:

```
ORDER BY table_name DESC;
```

While it's redundant, ASC may be used to specify ascending order. The following example sorts the table list first by tablespace name in descending order and then within that by table name in ascending order:

```
SELECT table_name, tablespace_name
FROM user_tables
ORDER BY tablespace_name DESC,
         table_name ASC;
```

If you want the sort to be case-insensitive, you can use Oracle's built-in UPPER function. For example:

```
SELECT table_name, tablespace_name
FROM user_tables
ORDER BY UPPER(table_name);
```

For symmetry, Oracle also has a built-in LOWER function. LOWER converts a string to lowercase; UPPER converts to uppercase.

Restricting query results

Use the WHERE clause to restrict the rows returned by a query to those that you need to see. The following example returns a list of any invalid objects that you own:

```
SELECT object_name, object_type
FROM user_objects
WHERE status = 'INVALID'
ORDER BY object_type, object_name;
```

The expression following the WHERE clause may be any valid Boolean expression. Oracle supports all the typical operators that you would expect: +, -, /, *, <, >, <>, <=, >=, AND, OR, NOT, ||, IS NULL, LIKE, BETWEEN, and IN. Parentheses are also supported and may be used to clarify the order of evaluation.

Null Values

Null values are pernicious, especially in the WHERE clause of a query. With only a few exceptions, any expression containing a null value will return a null as the result. Since nulls are considered neither true nor false, this can have unexpected ramifications in how a WHERE clause is evaluated. Consider the following query that attempts to retrieve a list of NUMBER columns with a scale other than 2:

```
SELECT table_name, column_name
FROM user_tab_columns
WHERE data_type = 'NUMBER'
AND data_scale <> 2;
```

This query is an utter failure because it misses all the floating-point NUMBER columns that have no scale defined at all. Avoid this problem by explicitly considering nulls when you write your WHERE clause. Use either the IS NULL or the IS NOT NULL operator. For example:

```
SELECT table_name, column_name
FROM user_tab_columns
WHERE data_type = 'NUMBER'
AND (data_scale <> 2
OR data_scale IS NULL);
```

When sorting data, null values are treated as greater than all other values. When a standard ascending sort is being done, null values will sort to the bottom of the list. A descending sort will cause null values to rise to the top. You can use the built-in NVL function to modify this behavior.

Using the NVL function

If you are returning results from a query that might be null, or you are sorting on results that might be null, you can use Oracle's built-in NVL function to replace null values with a selected non-null value. For example, the NUM_ROWS column in the USER_TABLES view will have a value only for tables that have been analyzed. Here, the NVL function is used to convert null values to zeros:

```
SELECT table_name, NVL(num_rows,0)
FROM user_tables
ORDER BY NVL(num_rows,0);
```

Be cautious about using NVL in a WHERE clause. Using NVL, or any other function, on an indexed column in a WHERE clause may prevent Oracle from using any index on that column.

Table Joins

It's very common to combine data from two or more tables in order to return related information. Such a combination of two tables is referred to as a *join*.

You join two tables by listing them in the FROM clause, separated by commas. For example:

```
SELECT user_constraints.constraint_name,
       user_constraints.constraint_type,
       user_cons_columns.column_name
  FROM user_constraints, user_cons_columns;
```

This query returns the *Cartesian product*—all possible combinations of all rows from both tables. Conceptually, this is where all joins start. In practice, you almost always put some conditions in the WHERE clause so that only related rows are combined. The following, more useful, query returns a list of constraint names together with the columns involved in each constraint:

```
SELECT user_constraints.constraint_name,
       user_constraints.constraint_type,
       user_cons_columns.column_name
  FROM user_constraints, user_cons_columns
 WHERE user_constraints.constraint_name
       = user_cons_columns.constraint_name;
```

Because both tables contain columns with matching names, the column references must be qualified with the table name. You can see that this quickly gets cumbersome. The

solution is to provide a shorter alias for each table and use
that alias to qualify the column names. For example:

```
SELECT uc.constraint_name,
       uc.constraint_type,
       ucc.column_name
FROM user_constraints uc,
     user_cons_columns ucc
WHERE uc.constraint_name =
   ucc.constraint_name;
```

Here, the alias uc is used for the user_constraints table,
while ucc is used for user_cons_columns. The resulting
query is much easier to read because you aren't over-
whelmed with long table names.

Inner and outer joins

The joins that you've seen so far are inner joins. An *inner
join* is one that returns data only when both tables have a
row that matches the join conditions. For example, the following query returns only tables that have constraints
defined on them:

```
SELECT ut.table_name, uc.constraint_name
FROM user_tables ut, user_constraints uc
WHERE ut.table_name = uc.table_name;
```

An *outer join* returns rows for one table, even when there
are no matching rows in the other. You specify an outer
join in Oracle by placing a plus sign (+) in parentheses following the column names from the optional table in your
WHERE clause. For example:

```
SELECT ut.table_name, uc.constraint_name
FROM user_tables ut, user_constraints uc
WHERE ut.table_name = uc.table_name(+);
```

The (+) following uc.table_name makes the user_constraint
table optional. The query will return all tables, and where
there are no corresponding constraint records, Oracle will
supply a null in the constraint name column.

Summary Queries

The GROUP BY and HAVING clauses, together with Oracle's built-in aggregate functions, allow you to summarize the data returned by a query.

Using aggregate functions

Aggregate functions take data from multiple rows as input and return one summarized value. For example, the following query uses the COUNT function to return the number of tables that you own:

```
SELECT COUNT(*)
FROM user_tables;
```

Oracle supports several different aggregate functions, all of which are listed in Table 1.

Table 1. Aggregate Functions

Function	Description
AVG	Averages the values in each group.
COUNT	Counts the non-null values in each group. COUNT(*) is a special case and counts all rows.
MAX	Returns the maximum value in a group.
MIN	Returns the minimum value in a group.
STDDEV	Returns the standard deviation of all values in a group.
SUM	Returns the sum of all values in a group.
VARIANCE	Returns the variance (related to standard deviation) of all values in a group.

Using GROUP BY

In addition to summarizing the entire results of a query, you can summarize the data for each distinct value in a column. For example, the following query returns the number of columns in each table you own:

```
SELECT ut.table_name, COUNT(utc.column_name)
FROM user_tables ut, user_tab_columns utc
WHERE ut.table_name = utc.table_name
GROUP BY ut.table_name
ORDER BY ut.table_name;
```

The following query extends the previous query and displays the number of columns in each table to which you have access. This time the grouping results in one row for each distinct owner and table name combination:

```
SELECT at.owner, at.table_name,
    COUNT(atc.column_name)
FROM all_tables at, all_tab_columns atc
WHERE at.table_name = atc.table_name
GROUP BY at.owner, at.table_name
ORDER BY at.owner, at.table_name;
```

If you want the results of a GROUP BY query returned in any particular order, you must include an ORDER BY clause. However, an ORDER BY clause is not required. At times it may appear that Oracle automatically sorts GROUP BY queries. It does, but only to a point. If you want the results sorted, you must include an ORDER BY clause.

Columns in the select list of a GROUP BY query must be either listed in the GROUP BY clause or enclosed by one of the aggregate functions listed earlier in Table 1.

Restricting summarized results

You can use the HAVING clause to restrict the rows returned by a summary query to only the rows of interest. The HAVING clause functions just like the WHERE clause, except that the HAVING conditions are applied to the summarized results. For example, the following query returns a list of all tables for which you have not defined any indexes:

```
SELECT ut.table_name, COUNT(ui.index_name)
FROM user_tables ut, user_indexes ui
WHERE ut.table_name = ui.table_name(+)
```

```
GROUP BY ut.table_name
HAVING COUNT(ui.index_name) = 0;
```

This query works by first counting up the number of index-es on each table and then eliminating those tables with nonzero counts.

Avoid placing conditions in the HAVING clause that do not test summarized values. Consider, for example, these two queries:

```
SELECT at.owner, at.table_name,
    COUNT(atc.column_name)
FROM all_tables at, all_tab_columns atc
WHERE at.table_name = atc.table_name
GROUP BY at.owner, at.table_name
HAVING at.owner <> 'SYS'
AND at.owner <> 'SYSTEM'
ORDER BY at.owner, at.table_name;

SELECT at.owner, at.table_name,
    COUNT(atc.column_name)
FROM all_tables at, all_tab_columns atc
WHERE at.table_name = atc.table_name
AND at.owner <> 'SYS'
AND at.owner <> 'SYSTEM'
GROUP BY at.owner, at.table_name
ORDER BY at.owner, at.table_name;
```

Both queries return the same result—a count of rows in each table except for those tables owned by SYS or SYSTEM. The second query, however, will execute more efficiently because tables owned by SYS and SYSTEM are eliminated by the WHERE clause before the data is summarized.

Using ALL and DISTINCT

The aggregate functions listed in Table 1 ignore null values. By default, they also exclude duplicate values. You can use the ALL and DISTINCT keywords to modify this behavior. For example:

```
SELECT COUNT (DISTINCT table_name)
FROM user_tab_columns;
SELECT COUNT (ALL table_name)
FROM user_tab_columns;
```

The first query uses the DISTINCT keyword to count up the number of tables. The second query uses the ALL keyword to count up the total number of columns defined for all those tables.

Unions

SQL supports four union operators that allow you to take the results of two queries and combine them into one. These are listed in Table 2.

Table 2. SQL's Union Operators

Function	Description
UNION	Combines the results of two queries and then eliminates duplicate rows.
UNION ALL	Combines the results of two queries without eliminating duplicate rows.
MINUS	Takes the rows returned by one query and eliminates those that are also returned by another.
INTERSECT	Takes the results from two queries and returns only rows that appear in both.

The following example of a union query uses the MINUS operator to return a list of all tables for which you have not yet defined any indexes:

```
SELECT table_name
FROM user_tables
MINUS
SELECT DISTINCT table_name
FROM user_indexes
WHERE table_owner = USER
ORDER BY table_name;
```

The first query returns a list of all tables you own. The second query returns a list of all tables that are indexed. The MINUS union operation removes those indexed tables from the first list, leaving only the unindexed tables.

NOTE

When two or more queries are unioned together, only one ORDER BY clause is allowed, and it must be at the end. Only the rows returned as the final result are sorted.

Formatting Reports

SQL*Plus reports are columnar in nature. SQL*Plus provides you with the ability to define column headings and display formats for each column in a report. You may also define page headers and footers, page and line breaks, and summary calculations such as totals and subtotals.

Column Headings

Specify column headings using the HEADING clause of the COLUMN command:

```
COLUMN employee_name HEADING "Employee Name"
```

Either single or double quotes may be used to enclose the heading text. The resulting heading will look like this:

```
Employee Name
- - - - - - - - - - - - -
```

To specify a multiline heading, use the vertical bar (|) character to specify the location of the line break. For example:

```
COLUMN employee_name HEADING "Employee|Name"
```

The resulting multiline heading will look like this:

```
Employee
Name
- - - - - - - - -
```

Headings of text columns are aligned to the left. Headings of numeric columns are aligned to the right. Use the JUSTIFY clause to alter that behavior:

```
COLUMN employee_name HEADING "Employee|Name" -
    JUSTIFY RIGHT
COLUMN employee_name HEADING "Employee|Name" -
    JUSTIFY CENTER
```

Use SET HEADSEP to change the line-break character to something other than a vertical bar. Use SET UNDERLINE to change the underline character to something other than a hyphen.

Column Formats

Specify display formats using the FORMAT clause of the COLUMN command. For numeric fields, format specifications can be quite detailed—controlling the length, the number of decimal places, and the punctuation used in the number. For text and date fields, you can control the column width and whether the column wraps. The "SQL*Plus Format Elements" section, later in this book, shows you how to format different types of data.

Page Width and Length

Page width is controlled by the SET LINESIZE command. The default width is 80 characters. You can change it—to 60 characters, for example—by using the command like this:

```
SET LINESIZE 60
```

The LINESIZE setting is used by SQL*Plus to center and right-justify page headers and page footers.

Page length is controlled by the SET PAGESIZE command. The default is to print 24 lines per page, and this includes the page header and page footer lines. The following command changes the page length to 50 lines:

```
SET PAGESIZE 50
```

Setting PAGESIZE to zero has a special meaning to SQL*Plus. A PAGESIZE of zero will inhibit the display of page headers, page footers, and column headings.

Page Headers and Footers

Define page headers and footers using the TTITLE and BTITLE commands. TTITLE, for top title, defines the page header. BTITLE, for bottom title, defines the page footer. The syntax is identical for both.

Defining a title

The following example defines a multiline page header with the company name on the left and the page number on the right:

```
TTITLE LEFT "My Company" CENTER "Current" -
RIGHT "Page" FORMAT 999 SQL.PNO SKIP 1 -
CENTER "Employee Listing" SKIP 4
```

The resulting title will look like this:

```
My Company          Current          Page    1
                 Employee Listing
```

The final SKIP clause provides three blank lines between the page title and the column headers. The same clauses work in the BTITLE command to define page footers.

Getting the date into a title

To get the current date into a page title, you must:

1. Get the date into a user variable.
2. Place the user variable into your BTITLE or TTITLE command.

You can use the following commands in a SQL*Plus script to get the current date into a user variable:

```
SET TERMOUT OFF
COLUMN curdate NEW_VALUE report_date
```

```
SELECT TO_CHAR(SYSDATE,'dd-Mon-yyyy') curdate
    FROM DUAL;
SET TERMOUT ON
```

After executing the commands shown here, the date will be in a user variable named REPORT_DATE. The following command places that value into a page footer:

```
BTITLE LEFT "Report Date: " report_date
```

This same technique can also be used to retrieve other values from the database and place them in either a page header or page footer.

Page Breaks

By default, SQL*Plus will print one blank line between each page of output. That blank line, added to the PAGESIZE setting, must equal the physical size of the pages in your printer.

The SET PAGESIZE command may be used to control the number of lines SQL*Plus prints on a page. SET NEWPAGE controls SQL*Plus' action when a page break occurs. You can change the number of blank lines between pages by using a command such as this:

```
SET NEWPAGE 10
```

You can tell SQL*Plus to display one form-feed character between pages by setting NEWPAGE to zero. For example:

```
SET NEWPAGE 0
```

Newer releases of SQL*Plus also allow SET NEWPAGE NONE, which eliminates both blank lines and form-feed characters from between pages.

Report Breaks

The BREAK and COMPUTE commands may be used to define breaks and summary calculations for a report. BREAK also allows you to inhibit the display of repetitive column values.

The BREAK command

To eliminate repetitive column values, use the BREAK command as shown in this example:

```
SQL> BREAK ON owner
SQL> SELECT owner, table_name
  2      FROM all_tables
  3  ORDER BY owner, table_name;

OWNER        TABLE_NAME
==========   ===============
CTXSYS       DR$CLASS
             DR$DELETE
             DR$INDEX
DEMO         CUSTOMER
             DEPARTMENT
             EMPLOYEE
```

When you list a column in the BREAK command, SQL*Plus prints the value of the column only when it changes. It's very important that you remember to sort the query results of the same column.

You can also use the BREAK command to skip lines or skip to a new page whenever a value changes. For example:

```
BREAK ON owner SKIP 1
BREAK ON owner SKIP PAGE
```

The first command results in printing a blank line whenever the owner changes. The second results in a page break each time the owner changes.

Multiple breaks may be specified for a report, but that's always done using just one command. The following example causes a page break to occur whenever an owner changes and a blank line to be printed whenever the object type changes:

```
BREAK ON owner SKIP PAGE ON object_type SKIP 1
SELECT owner, object_type, object_name
    FROM dba_objects
ORDER BY owner, object_type, object_name;
```

Before performing the break actions for a column, SQL*Plus will first perform the break actions for all inner columns. In this case, a change in the owner field would result in one skipped line and *then* a page break.

The COMPUTE command

The COMPUTE command tells SQL*Plus to compute summary values for a group of records. COMPUTE is always used in tandem with BREAK. For example, to compute the number of tables owned by each user, you could do the following:

```
BREAK ON owner
COMPUTE COUNT OF table_name ON owner
SELECT owner, table_name
    FROM dba_tables
ORDER BY owner, table_name;
```

SQL*Plus counts the number of table names for each distinct owner value and displays the results whenever a break occurs in the owner field.

You can compute summaries on multiple columns at once by using multiple COMPUTE commands. The following example counts the number of objects of each type and sums the extent sizes for each object:

```
COMPUTE SUM OF bytes -
    ON segment_name
COMPUTE COUNT OF segment_name -
    ON segment_type
BREAK ON segment_type ON segment_name
SELECT segment_name, segment_type, bytes
    FROM user_extents
ORDER BY segment_type, segment_name;
```

Notice that the display order—the order used in the SELECT list—does not need to match the sort order or the break order. Also notice that multiple summaries are defined using multiple COMPUTE commands, but multiple breaks are defined using just one BREAK command.

Tuning SQL

SQL*Plus can be employed as a tool to help tune SQL statements. You can use SQL's EXPLAIN PLAN facility to get the execution plan for a statement into a table. Then you can query that table by using SQL*Plus to display that plan. If you don't like the plan that Oracle is using, you can add optimizer hints to your SQL statement that specify how you want the statement to be executed.

Creating the Plan Table

Before you can use the EXPLAIN PLAN statement, you need to create a plan table to hold the results. Oracle provides a script named *utlxplan.sql* to create the plan table, and you'll find it in the *$ORACLE_HOME/rdbms/admin* directory. Execute it as follows:

```
SQL> @e:\oracle\ora81\rdbms\admin\utlxplan

Table created.
```

The resulting table, PLAN_TABLE, looks like this:

Name	Null?	Type
STATEMENT_ID		VARCHAR2(30)
TIMESTAMP		DATE
REMARKS		VARCHAR2(80)
OPERATION		VARCHAR2(30)
OPTIONS		VARCHAR2(30)
OBJECT_NODE		VARCHAR2(128)
OBJECT_OWNER		VARCHAR2(30)
OBJECT_NAME		VARCHAR2(30)
OBJECT_INSTANCE		NUMBER(38)
OBJECT_TYPE		VARCHAR2(30)
OPTIMIZER		VARCHAR2(255)
SEARCH_COLUMNS		NUMBER
ID		NUMBER(38)
PARENT_ID		NUMBER(38)
POSITION		NUMBER(38)
COST		NUMBER(38)

```
CARDINALITY                    NUMBER(38)
BYTES                          NUMBER(38)
OTHER_TAG                      VARCHAR2(255)
PARTITION_START                VARCHAR2(255)
PARTITION_STOP                 VARCHAR2(255)
PARTITION_ID                   NUMBER(38)
OTHER                          LONG
DISTRIBUTION                   VARCHAR2(30)
```

The columns in the plan table often vary from one release of Oracle to the next. This version of the plan table is from Oracle8*i* release 8.1.5.

Explaining a Query

Use the EXPLAIN PLAN statement to get the execution plan for a SQL statement. Oracle will place the execution plan into the plan table that you've created.

EXPLAIN PLAN syntax

The syntax for EXPLAIN PLAN looks like this:

```
EXPLAIN PLAN
        [SET STATEMENT_ID = 'statement_id']
        [INTO table_name]
        FOR statement;
```

The parameters follow:

statement_id

Identifies the query you are explaining and is stored in the STATEMENT_ID field of the plan table records. This defaults to null.

table_name

Is the name of the plan table and defaults to PLAN_ TABLE.

statement

Is the SELECT, INSERT, UPDATE, or DELETE statement to be explained.

EXPLAIN PLAN example

First, delete any existing plan table records with the statement ID you are about to use. For example:

```
DELETE FROM plan_table
WHERE statement_id = 'HOURS_BY_PROJECT';
```

Insert the EXPLAIN PLAN statement onto the front of the SQL statement that you are interested in explaining, then execute the resulting, longer statement. For example:

```
EXPLAIN PLAN
SET STATEMENT_ID = 'HOURS_BY_PROJECT'
FOR
SELECT employee_name, project_name,
       SUM(hours_logged)
FROM employee, project, project_hours
WHERE employee.employee_id
       = project_hours.employee_id
   AND project.project_id
       = project_hours.project_id
GROUP BY employee_name, project_name;
```

Your next step is to query the plan table for the results.

Querying the Plan Table

The typical way to look at an execution plan is to display it using a hierarchical query. Oracle breaks query execution down into a series of nested steps, each of which feeds data up to a parent step. The ultimate parent is the query itself; the output of which is returned to the application. The typical query used to display plan output looks like this:

```
SELECT LPAD(' ', 2*(level-1)) ||
       operation || ' ' || options
       || ' ' || object_name || ' ' ||
       DECODE(id, 0, 'Cost = ' || position)
       "Query Plan"
FROM plan_table
START WITH id = 0 AND statement_id
              = 'HOURS_BY_PROJECT'
CONNECT BY prior id = parent_id
       AND statement_id = 'HOURS_BY_PROJECT';
```

The result of this query will be a report showing the steps in the execution plan, with each child step indented underneath its parent, as shown in this example:

```
Query Plan
-----------------------------------------
SELECT STATEMENT    Cost = 7
   SORT GROUP BY
      HASH JOIN
         HASH JOIN
            TABLE ACCESS FULL EMPLOYEE
            TABLE ACCESS FULL PROJECT_HOURS
         TABLE ACCESS FULL PROJECT
```

The cost for one execution plan can only be interpreted relative to another. A statement with a cost of 14 would require twice the I/O and CPU resources of a query with a cost of 7.

WARNING

Statistics are required to compute a cost. Out-of-date statistics will result in an inaccurate cost.

Table 3 describes the various plan operations and their options.

Table 3. EXPLAIN PLAN Operations

Operation and Options	Description
AND-EQUAL	Has two or more child steps, each of which returns a set of ROWIDs. The AND-EQUAL operation selects only those ROWIDs that are returned by all the child operations.
BITMAP CONVERSION TO ROWIDS	Converts a bitmap from a bitmap index to a set of ROWIDs that can be used to retrieve the actual data.

Table 3. EXPLAIN PLAN Operations (continued)

Operation and Options	Description
BITMAP CONVERSION FROM ROWIDS	Converts a set of ROWIDs into a bitmapped representation.
BITMAP CONVERSION COUNT	Counts the number of rows represented by a bitmap.
BITMAP INDEX SINGLE VALUE	Retrieves the bitmap for a single key value.
BITMAP INDEX RANGE SCAN	Returns the bitmaps for a range of key values.
BITMAP INDEX FULL	Scans an entire bitmapped index.
BITMAP MERGE	Merges two bitmaps together, using an OR operation, and returns one bitmap as the result.
BITMAP MINUS	Subtracts one bitmap index from another. Rows represented by the second bitmap are excluded from the result.
BITMAP OR	Merges two bitmaps together using an OR operation.
CONNECT BY	Retrieves rows hierarchically and is the result of a query written with a CONNECT BY clause.
CONCATENA-TION	Combines multiple sets of rows into one set; essentially a UNION ALL.
COUNT	Counts the number of rows that have been selected from a table.
COUNT STOPKEY	Counts the number of rows up to the number specified for ROWNUM in the query's WHERE clause.
FILTER	Filters a set of rows based on a condition from a query's WHERE clause.

Table 3. EXPLAIN PLAN Operations (continued)

Operation and Options	Description
FIRST ROW	Retrieves only the first row of a query's result set.
FOR UPDATE	Locks rows that are retrieved. This would be the result of specifying FOR UPDATE in the original query.
HASH JOIN	Joins two tables using a hash join method.
INDEX UNIQUE	Looks up a value using a unique index.
INDEX RANGE SCAN	Scans an index for a range of values.
INDEX RANGE SCAN DESCENDING	Performs the same function as INDEX RANGE SCAN, but the index is scanned in descending order.
INLIST ITERATOR	Performs one or more operations once for each value in an IN predicate.
INTERSECTION	Takes two rowsets as input and returns only rows that appear in both.
MERGE JOIN	Joins two rowsets based on some common value. Both rowsets will first have been sorted by this value. This is an inner join.
MERGE JOIN OUTER	Performs a function similar to a MERGE JOIN, but an outer join is performed.
MERGE JOIN ANTI	Indicates that an anti-join is being performed.
MERGE JOIN SEMI	Indicates that a semi-join is being performed.
MINUS	Takes two rowsets as inputs and returns rows from the first set that do not appear in the second.

Table 3. EXPLAIN PLAN Operations (continued)

Operation and Options	Description
NESTED LOOPS	Uses a nested loop to perform an operation (usually a join) for all combinations of rows from two rowsets.
NESTED LOOPS OUTER	Performs the same function as NESTED LOOPS but indicates an outer join.
PARTITION	Executes an operation for one or more partitions. The PARTITION_ START and PARTITION_STOP columns give the range of partitions over which the operation is performed.
PARTITION SINGLE	Executes an operation on a single partition.
PARTITION ITERATOR	Executes an operation on several partitions.
PARTITION ALL	Executes an operation on all partitions.
PARTITION INLIST	Performs the same function as PARTITION ITERATOR, but the list of partitions is being driven by an IN predicate.
PROJECTION	Takes multiple queries as input and returns a single set of records. This is used with INTERSECTION, MINUS, and UNION operations.
REMOTE	Indicates that a rowset is being returned from a remote database.
SEQUENCE	Indicates that an Oracle sequence is being accessed.
SORT AGGREGATE	Applies a group function, such as COUNT, to a rowset and returns only one row as the result.

Table 3. EXPLAIN PLAN Operations (continued)

Operation and Options	Description
SORT UNIQUE	Sorts a rowset and eliminates duplicates.
SORT GROUP BY	Sorts a rowset into groups. This is the result of a GROUP BY clause.
SORT JOIN	Sorts a rowset in preparation for a join. See MERGE JOIN.
SORT ORDER BY	Sorts a rowset in accordance with the ORDER BY clause specified in the query.
TABLE ACCESS FULL	Reads all rows in the specified table.
TABLE ACCESS CLUSTER	Reads all rows in a table that match a specified index cluster key.
TABLE ACCESS HASH	Reads all rows in a table that match a specified hash cluster key.
TABLE ACCESS BY ROWID	Retrieves a row from a table based on its ROWID.
UNION	Takes two rowsets, eliminates duplicates, and returns the result as one set.
VIEW	Executes the query behind a view and returns the resulting rowset.

Using Optimizer Hints

Rather than allow Oracle to have total control over how a query is executed, you can provide specific directions to the optimizer through the use of hints. A *hint*, in Oracle, is an optimizer directive that is embedded in a SQL statement in the form of a comment. For example, here is a query with an optimizer hint telling Oracle to do a full table scan:

```
SELECT /*+ FULL(employee) */
       employee_id,
```

```
        employee_name,
        employee_billing_rate
    FROM employee
    WHERE employee_name = 'Jenny Gennick';
```

The hint in this case is FULL(employee) telling Oracle to do a full table scan of the employee table. Oracle will honor this hint and perform a full table scan even if there happens to be an index on the employee name field.

Hints must be in a comment of the form /*+...*/, and that comment must follow the SQL keyword that begins the statement.

Optimizer hints can be divided into the following five categories: optimizer goal hints, access method hints, join order hints, join operation hints, and parallel execution hints.

Optimizer goal hints

Optimizer goal hints allow you to influence the optimizer's overall goal when formulating an execution plan:

ALL_ROWS
    Produce an execution plan that minimizes resource consumption.

FIRST_ROWS
    Produce an execution plan that gets to the first row as fast as possible.

CHOOSE
    Use the cost-based optimizer if statistics are present for at least one of the tables referenced in a query.

RULE
    Use the rules-based optimizer.

Access method hints

Access method hints allow you to control the manner in which Oracle accesses data:

FULL(*table_name*)

Do a full table scan of the specified table.

ROWID(*table_name*)

Scan the specified table based on ROWIDs.

CLUSTER(*table_name*)

Do a cluster scan of the specified table.

HASH(*table_name*)

Do a hash scan of the specified table.

HASH_AJ(*table_name*)

Do a hash anti-join of the specified table.

INDEX(*table_name* [*index_name* ...])

Access the specified table via an index scan. Optionally, you may specify a list of indexes from which to choose.

INDEX_ASC(*table_name* [*index_name* ...])

Perform the same function as INDEX, but scan in ascending order.

INDEX_COMBINE(*table_name* [*index_name* ...])

Use some combination of two indexes. You may optionally specify a list of indexes to use.

INDEX_DESC(*table_name* [*index_name* ...])

Perform the same function as INDEX, but scan in descending order.

INDEX_FFS(*table_name* [*index_name* ...])

Do a fast full index scan.

MERGE_AJ(*table_name*)

Turn a NOT IN subquery into a merge anti-join.

AND_EQUAL(*table_name* *index_name* *index_name* ...)

Scan two or more indexes and merge the results. You must specify at least two index names.

USE_CONCAT

Turn a query with OR conditions into two or more queries unioned together with a UNION ALL.

Join order hints

Join order hints allow you to exercise some control over the order in which tables are joined:

ORDERED
> Join tables left to right in the same order in which they are listed in the FROM clause.

STAR
> Use a star query execution plan, if at all possible. This can work only if there are at least three tables being joined and if the largest table has a concatenated index on columns that reference the two smaller tables. The two smaller tables are joined first, and then a nested-loop join is used to retrieve the required rows from the largest table.

STAR_TRANSFORMATION
> Transform the query into a star query, if possible, and then use the best plan for that query.

Join operation hints

Join operation hints allow you to control the manner in which two tables are joined:

USE_NL(*table_name*)
> Use a nested loop when joining this table. The table specified by this hint will be the one accessed by the innermost loop. The other table will be the driving table.

USE_MERGE(*table_name*)
> Use the sort merge method when joining this table.

USE_HASH(*table_name*)
> Use a hash join for the specified table.

NO_MERGE
> Prevent Oracle from merging the query from a view into the main query.

DRIVING_SITE(*table_name*)
> Drive a distributed join from the site where the named table resides.

Parallel execution hints

Parallel execution hints influence the way in which Oracle uses the resources of a parallel processing environment to execute a query:

PARALLEL(*table_name*[, *degree*[, *num_instances*]])
> Access data from the indicated table in a parallel processing mode. You can optionally specify both the degree of parallelism to use and the number of instances that will be involved. The DEFAULT keyword may be used for both arguments, in which case Oracle decides the values based on parameters in the *INIT.ORA* file.

NO_PARALLEL(*table_name*)
> Do not access the specified table in parallel.

APPEND
> Do not attempt to reuse any free space that may be available in any extents currently allocated to the table. Applies only to INSERT statements.

NOAPPEND
> Use any free space in extents currently allocated to the table. Applies only to INSERT statements.

PARALLEL_INDEX(*table_name*, *index_name* [,*degree*
[,*num_instances*]])
> Access data from the indicated table by scanning the specified index in a parallel processing mode. The index must be a partitioned index. You can optionally specify both the degree of parallelism to use and the number of instances that will be involved. The DEFAULT keyword may be used for both arguments, in which case Oracle decides the values based on parameters in the *INIT.ORA* file.

CACHE(*table_name*)
> Place blocks for the table at the most recently used end of the buffer cache, so that they will remain in memory as long as possible.

NOCACHE(*table_name*)

Place blocks at the least recently used end of the buffer cache, where they will be cleared out as soon as possible.

PUSH_SUBQ

Evaluate nonmerged subqueries as soon as possible during query execution. If you expect the subquery to eliminate a large number of rows, this can result in a performance improvement.

SQL*Plus Format Elements

The COLUMN, ACCEPT, SET NUMBER, TTITLE, BTITLE, REPHEADER, and REPFOOTER commands allow you to control data formats using what is called a format specification. A *format specification* is a string of characters that tells SQL*Plus exactly how to format a number, date, or text string when it is displayed.

Formatting Numbers

Table 4 shows the format elements that may be used when formatting numeric output.

Table 4. Numeric Format Elements

Format Element	Function
9	Represents a digit in the output.
0	Marks the spot at which you want to begin displaying leading zeros.
$	Includes a leading dollar sign in the output.
,	Places a comma in the output.
.	Marks the location of the decimal point.
B	Forces zero values to be displayed as blanks.
MI	Adds a trailing negative sign to a number and may be used only at the end of a format string.
S	Adds a + or - sign[a] to the number and may be used at either the beginning or end of a format string.

Table 4. Numeric Format Elements (continued)

Format Element	Function
PR	Causes negative values to be displayed within angle brackets. For example, −123.99 will be displayed as <123.99>.
D	Marks the location of the decimal point.
G	Places a group separator (usually a comma) in the output.
C	Marks the place where you want the ISO currency indicator to appear. For U.S. dollars, this will be USD.
L	Marks the place where you want the local currency indicator to appear. For U.S. dollars, this will be the dollar sign character.
V	Displays scaled values. The number of digits to the right of the V indicates how many places to the right the decimal point is shifted before the number is displayed.
EEEE	Causes SQL*Plus to use scientific notation to display a value. You must use exactly four Es, and they must appear at the right end of the format string.
RN	Allows you to display a number using Roman numerals. An uppercase RN yields uppercase Roman numerals, while a lowercase rn yields lowercase Roman numerals. Numbers displayed as Roman numerals must be integers and must be between 1 and 3,999, inclusive.
DATE	Causes SQL*Plus to assume that the number represents a Julian date and to display it in MM/DD/YY format.

[a] SQL*Plus always allows for a sign somewhere when you display a number. The default is for the sign to be positioned to the left of the number and to be displayed only when the number is negative. Positive numbers will have a blank space in the leftmost position.

Table 5 contains several examples illustrating the use of the various format elements.

Table 5. Numeric Format Examples

Value	Format	Result
123	9999	123
1234.01	9,999.99	1,234.01
23456	$999,999.99	$23,456.00
1	0999	0001
1	99099	001
-1000.01	9,999.99mi	1,000.01-
1001	S9,999	+1,001
-1001	9,999PR	<1,001>
1001	9,999PR	1,001

Formatting Character Strings

Character strings are formatted using only one element. That element is "A", and it is followed by a number specifying the column width in terms of characters. For example:

```
SQL> COLUMN a FORMAT A40
SQL> SELECT 'An apple a day keeps the doctor
    away.' A
    2    FROM dual;

A
----------------------------------------
An apple a day keeps the doctor away.
```

By default, longer text values are wrapped within the column. You can use the WORD_WRAPPED, WRAPPED, and TRUNCATED parameters of the COLUMN command to control whether and how wrapping occurs. For example:

```
SQL> COLUMN a FORMAT A18 WORD_WRAPPED
SQL> SELECT 'An apple a day keeps the doctor
    away.' A
    2    FROM dual;
```

```
A
-----------------
An apple a day
keeps the doctor
away.
```

When text columns wrap to multiple lines, SQL*Plus will print a blank line called a *record separator* following the record. Use SET RECSEP OFF to prevent that behavior.

When used with the ACCEPT command, a character format defines the maximum number of characters SQL*Plus will accept from the user.

Formatting Dates

The date format elements in Table 6 may be used with Oracle's built-in TO_CHAR function to convert date values to character strings. For example:

```
SQL> SELECT TO_CHAR(SYSDATE,
  2 'dd-Mon-yyyy hh:mi:ss PM')
  3    FROM dual;

TO_CHAR(SYSDATE,'DD-MON
-----------------------
13-Dec-1999 09:13:59 PM
```

When used with the ACCEPT command, a date format string requires the user to enter a date in the format specified.

Table 6. Date Format Elements

Format Element	Function
-/,.;:	Punctuation to be included in the output.
'text'	Quoted text to be reproduced in the output.
AD or A.D. BC or B.C.	An AD or BC indicator included with the date.

Table 6. Date Format Elements (continued)

Format Element	Function
AM or A.M. PM or P.M.	AM or PM printed, whichever applies given the time in question.
CC	The century number. This will be 20 for years 1900 through 1999.
SCC	Same as CC, but negative for BC dates.
D	The number of the day of the week. This will be one through seven.
DAY	The full name of the day.
DD	The day of the month.
DDD	The day of the year.
DY	The abbreviated name of the day.
HH	The hour of the day on a 12-hour clock.
HH12	The hour of the day on a 12-hour clock.
HH24	The hour of the day on a 24-hour clock.
IW	The week of the year. This will be 1–53.
IYYY	The four-digit year.
IYY	The last three digits of the year number.
IY	The last two digits of the year number.
I	The last digit of the year number.
J	The Julian day. Day one is equivalent to Jan 1, 4712 BC.
MI	The minute.
MM	The month number.
MON	The three-letter month abbreviation.
MONTH	The month name, fully spelled out.
Q	The quarter of the year. Quarter one is Jan–Mar; quarter two is Apr–Jun; and so forth.
RM	The month number in Roman numerals.
RR	The last two digits of the year.
RRRR	The four-digit year.

Table 6. Date Format Elements (continued)

Format Element	Function
SS	The second.
SSSSS	The number of seconds since midnight.
WW	The week of the year.
W	The week of the month. Week one starts on the first of the month; week two starts on the eighth of the month; and so forth.
Y,YYY	The four-digit year with a comma after the first digit.
YEAR	The year spelled out in words.
SYEAR	The year spelled out in words with a leading negative sign when the year is BC.
YYYY	The four-digit year.
SYYYY	The four-digit year with a leading negative sign when the year is BC.
YYY	The last three digits of the year number.
YY	The last two digits of the year number.
Y	The last digit of the year number.

When you use a date format element that displays a text value, such as the name of a month, the case used for the format element drives the case used in the output. Table 7 shows examples of formatting dates.

Table 7. Date Format Examples

Format	Result
dd-mon-yyyy	13-dec-1999
dd-Mon-yyyy	13-Dec-1999
DD-MON-YYYY	13-DEC-1999
Month dd, yyyy	December 13, 1999
mm/dd/yyyy	12/13/1999
Day	Sunday

SQL*Plus Command Reference

This chapter contains an alphabetic listing of all of the SQL*Plus commands, with brief descriptions.

Comment Delimiters (/*...*/)

```
/*
comment_text
comment_text
comment_text
*/
```

The /* and */ delimiters may be used to set off a comment in SQL*Plus. Comments entered this way may span multiple lines. If you use /*...*/ in a script file, the comments will be displayed on the screen when the script is executed. For example:

```
/* SQL*Plus script written 7-Jan-2000
   by Jonathan Gennick. */
```

Double Hyphen (--)

```
--comment_text
```

The double hyphen may be used to place a single-line comment in a SQL*Plus script. For example:

```
--Written 7-Jan-2000 by Jonathan Gennick
```

At Sign (@)

```
@script_file [argument...]
```

The at sign is used to execute a SQL*Plus script file. For example:

```
@$ORACLE_HOME/rdbms/admin/utlxplan
```

```
@add_user "TINA" "SECRETPASSWORD"
```

Parameters

script_file

> Is the name of the file to execute. You may include a path as part of the name. If you do not specify a path, SQL*Plus will look in the current directory and then follow the SQL*Plus search path. The default extension is *.sql.*

argument

> Is an argument you wish to pass to the script. You may pass as many arguments as the script requires. Arguments must be separated from each other by at least one space.

Double At Sign (@@)

```
@@script_file [argument...]
```

The double at sign is used within a script file to execute another script file from the same directory as the first. For example:

```
@@generate_emp_report
@@generate_pay_history_report '101'
```

The parameters for @@ are the same as for @.

Forward Slash (/)

```
/
```

A forward slash is used to execute the SQL statement or PL/SQL block that is currently in the buffer. For example:

```
SQL> SELECT * FROM dual
  2
SQL> /

D
-
X
```

ACCEPT

```
ACC[EPT] user_variable [NUM[BER] | CHAR | DATE]
    [FOR[MAT] format_specification]
    [DEF[AULT] default_value]
    [PROMPT prompt_text | NOPR[OMPT]]
    [HIDE]
```

The ACCEPT command is used to get input from a user. For example:

```
ACCEPT user_password CHAR -
    PROMPT "Password: " HIDE
ACCEPT id NUMBER FORMAT "999.99"
ACCEPT report_date DATE -
    PROMPT "Date: " FORMAT "dd-mon-yyyy"
```

Parameters

user_variable

Is the name of the variable that you want to define.

NUM[BER] | CHAR | DATE

Is the type of data you are after.

FOR[MAT] *format_specification*

Is a format specification, which may be optionally enclosed in quotes.

DEF[AULT] *default_value*

Specifies a default value to assign to the variable.

PROMPT *prompt_text*

Is the prompt text displayed to the user.

NOPR[OMPT]

Indicates that you do not want the user to see a visible prompt.

HIDE

Causes SQL*Plus not to echo the user's response back to the display. This is useful if you are prompting for a password.

The syntax for the ACCEPT command has evolved significantly with the past few releases of SQL*Plus. The syntax shown here is valid for version 8.1. Not all of the clauses are available when using prior versions.

APPEND

    A[PPEND] text

APPEND is an editing command that lets you add text onto the end of the current line in the SQL buffer. For example:

    SQL> L
      1* SELECT *
    SQL> a   FROM dual
      1* SELECT * FROM dual

The *text* is the text you want appended to the current line.

NOTE

Use two spaces after the APPEND command if you want your appended string to begin with one space.

ARCHIVE LOG

    ARCHIVE LOG {LIST |
                STOP |
                START [TO destination] |
                NEXT [TO destination] |
                ALL [TO destination] |
                log_sequence_number [TO
                    destination]}

The ARCHIVE LOG command is used to control—or display information about—archive logging. You must be connected as SYSDBA, SYSOPER, or INTERNAL in order to use this command. For example:

```
ARCHIVE LOG LIST
ARCHIVE LOG START
ARCHIVE LOG ALL TO /m01/oradata
```

Parameters

LIST

Causes SQL*Plus to display information about the current state of archiving.

STOP

Stops log files from being automatically archived.

START

Turns on automatic archiving of redo log files.

NEXT

Manually archives the next log file group in the sequence, provided that it is filled. Use ARCHIVE LOG LIST to see the sequence number of this file.

ALL

Manually archives all log file groups that have been filled but not previously archived.

log_sequence_number

Manually archives a specific log file group, provided that the group is still online.

destination

Specifies a destination for archived log files. If used with ARCHIVE LOG START, this becomes the destination for all log files as they are archived. If used with NEXT, ALL, or a specific sequence number, this becomes the destination for files archived by that one command. If you do not specify a destination when using ARCHIVE LOG START, the value from the LOG_ARCHIVE_ DEST initialization parameter is used.

ATTRIBUTE

```
ATTRIBUTE [object_type.attribute |
          attribute_alias
          [ALI[AS] alias | CLE[AR]|
          FOR[MAT] format_spec |
          LIKE source_attribute |
          ON | OFF...]]
```

The ATTRIBUTE command is used to format attributes of an Oracle8 object type. For example:

```
ATTRIBUTE employee_type.employee_salary -
   ALIAS emp_sal
ATTRIBUTE emp_sal FORMAT "$999,999.99"
ATTRIBUTE employee_type.employee_salary -
   FORMAT "$999,999.99"
```

Issuing the ATTRIBUTE command with no parameters gets you a list of all current attribute settings.

Parameters

object_type

Is the name of an Oracle8 object type.

attribute

Is the name of an attribute of the specified object type and is the attribute you are formatting. If you stop here and don't supply any other parameters, the current display settings for this attribute are shown.

The ALIAS, CLEAR, FORMAT, LIKE, ON, and OFF clauses function just as they do in the COLUMN command.

BREAK

```
BRE[AK] [ON {column_name | ROW | REPORT}
        [SKI[P] {lines_to_skip | PAGE} |
        NODUP[LICATES] |
        DUP[LICATES]...]...]
```

The BREAK command is used to define page breaks and line breaks based on changing column values in a report. It controls whether duplicate values print in a column, and it controls the printing of computed values such as totals and subtotals. Issuing the BREAK command with no parameters causes SQL*Plus to display the current break setting. For example:

```
BREAK ON ROW SKIP 1
BREAK ON dept
BREAK ON dept SKIP PAGE
```

Parameters

column_name

Specifies a report column to watch. When the value in the column changes, SQL*Plus executes the specified break actions.

ROW

Causes SQL*Plus to break on each row.

REPORT

Specifies a report-level break and is used to cause SQL*Plus to print grand totals at the end of the report. SKIP PAGE will be ignored if it is specified as a report break action, but, strangely enough, you can skip lines on a report break.

SKI[P] *lines_to_skip*

Tells SQL*Plus to skip the specified number of lines when a break occurs.

SKI[P] PAGE

Tells SQL*Plus to advance to a new page when a break occurs.

NODUP[LICATES]

Tells SQL*Plus to print a column's value only when it changes. By default, whenever you put a break on a column, you get this behavior.

DUP[LICATES]

Forces SQL*Plus to print a column's value in every line on the report, regardless of whether the value is the same as that printed for the previous record.

BTITLE

```
BTI[TLE] [[OFF | ON] |
    COL x | S[KIP] x |
    TAB x | LE[FT] |
    CE[NTER] | R[IGHT] |
    BOLD | FOR[MAT] format_spec |
    text | variable...]
```

See TTITLE for descriptions of the command parameters. BTITLE functions the same as TTITLE, except that it defines a page footer instead of a page header.

CHANGE

```
C[HANGE] /old_text[/[new_text[/]]
```

CHANGE is an editing command that allows you to do a search and replace on the current line in the SQL buffer. The CHANGE command is also used to delete text. For example:

```
SQL> l
  1* SELECT dummy,smarty FROM duap
SQL> c /duap/dual/
  1* SELECT dummy,smarty FROM dual
SQL> c /,smarty/
  1* SELECT dummy FROM dual
```

Parameters

old_text

Is the text you want to change or delete.

new_text

Is the replacement text.

/ Commonly used to delimit the old and new text strings, but any other character may be used as long as it is not a number or letter—and as long as it is used consistently throughout the command.

CLEAR

```
CL[EAR] {BRE[AKS] | BUFF[ER] | COL[UMNS] |
    COMP[UTES] | SCR[EEN] | SQL | TIMI[NG]}
```

The CLEAR command allows you to easily delete all column definitions, break settings, compute definitions, and so forth. For example:

```
CLEAR BREAKS
CLEAR COMPUTES
```

Parameters

BRE[AKS]

Deletes any break setting you may have defined using the BREAK command.

BUFF[ER]

Erases the contents of the buffer.

COL[UMNS]

Deletes any column definitions you may have made using the COLUMN command.

COMP[UTES]

Deletes any computations you may have defined using the COMPUTE command.

SCR[EEN]

Clears the screen.

SQL

Erases the contents of the SQL buffer.

TIMI[NG]

Deletes any timers you may have created using the TIMING command.

COLUMN

```
COL[UMN] [column_name [ALI[AS] alias |
    CLE[AR] | FOLD_A[FTER] | FOLD_B[EFORE] |
    FOR[MAT] format_spec | HEA[DING]
        heading_text |
    JUS[TIFY] {LEFT | CENTER | CENTRE | RIGHT} |
    LIKE source_column_name | NEWL[INE] |
    NEW_V[ALUE] user_variable | NOPRI[NT] |
    PRI[NT] | NUL[L] null_text |
    OLD_V[ALUE] user_variable | ON | OFF |
    TRU[NCATED] | WOR[D_WRAPPED] |
        WRA[PPED]...]]
```

The COLUMN command is used to format report output for columnar reports. Issuing the COLUMN command with no parameters gets you a list of all current column formats. For example:

```
COLUMN employee_name HEADING "Name" -
    FORMAT A20 WORD_WRAPPED
COLUMN employee_hire_date -
    HEADING "Hire Date" -
    FORMAT A12 JUSTIFY RIGHT
```

COLUMN commands are cumulative. Two COLUMN commands specifying two different settings for the same field are equivalent to one command specifying both parameters.

Parameters

column_name

Is the name of the column you are formatting. If it is a computed column, the expression is the name. If your SELECT statement aliases the column, you must use that alias name here. Issuing the command COLUMN *column_name* with no further parameters causes SQL*Plus to display the current format for that column.

ALI[AS]

Allows you to specify an alternate name for this column that is meaningful to SQL*Plus.

alias

Is an alternate name for the column that may be used in BREAK commands, COMPUTE commands, and other COLUMN commands.

CLE[AR]

Erases any format settings for the column in question.

FOLD_A[FTER]

Causes SQL*Plus to advance to a new line after printing this column.

FOLD_B[EFORE]

Causes SQL*Plus to wrap to a new line before this column is printed.

FOR[MAT]

Allows you to control how the data for the column is displayed.

format_spec

Is a string that specifies the display format for the column.

HEA[DING]

Allows you to define a heading for the column.

heading_text

Is the text you want for the column heading. This may optionally be enclosed in either single or double quotes.

JUS[TIFY] {LEFT | CENTER | CENTRE | RIGHT}

Controls where the heading text prints relative to the column width. By default, headings for numeric fields print flush right, and headings for text fields print flush left. This parameter allows you to change that behavior.

LIKE

Causes the column to be defined with the same format attributes as another column.

---

source_column_name

Is the name of the source column used with the LIKE parameter.

NEWL[INE]

Causes SQL*Plus to wrap to a new line before the column is printed.

NEW_V[ALUE]

Causes SQL*Plus to keep a user variable updated with the current value of the column.

user_variable

Is the name of a user variable for use with the NEW_VALUE and OLD_VALUE parameters.

NOPRI[NT]

Tells SQL*Plus not to print the column.

PRI[NT]

Enables the printing of a column.

NUL[L]

Allows you to specify text to be displayed when the column value is null.

null_text

Is the text you want displayed when the column in question is null.

OLD_V[ALUE]

Causes SQL*Plus to keep a user variable updated with the previous value of the column.

ON

Causes SQL*Plus to print the column using the format you have specified. This is the default behavior.

OFF

Disables the format settings for the column.

TRU[NCATED]

Causes the column text to be truncated to the width of the column. Longer values are not wrapped.

WOR[D_WRAPPED]

Causes SQL*Plus to word-wrap long column values.

WRA[PPED]

Causes SQL*Plus to wrap long column values. Line breaks occur exactly at the column boundary, even in the middle of a word.

COMPUTE

```
COMP[UTE] [{AVG | COU[NT] | MAX[IMUM] |
          MIN[IMUM] | NUM[BER] | STD | SUM |
          VAR[IANCE]}]...
[LABEL label_text]
          OF column_name...
          ON {group_column_name |
             ROW | REPORT}...]
```

The COMPUTE command defines summary calculations needed in a report. You can use COMPUTE in conjunction with BREAK to calculate and print column totals, averages, minimum and maximum values, and so forth. These calculations are performed by SQL*Plus as the report runs. COMPUTE is a complex command and must be used in conjunction with the BREAK command in order to get results. For example:

```
BREAK ON project_id
COMPUTE SUM LABEL "Totals" OF hours_logged -
   ON project_id

BREAK ON project_id ON employee_id
COMPUTE SUM OF hours_logged -
   ON project_id, employee_id
```

Issuing COMPUTE with no parameters causes SQL*Plus to list all currently defined computations.

Parameters

AVG

Computes the average of all non-null values for a numeric column.

COU[NT]

Computes the total number of non-null values for a column.

MAX[IMUM]

Computes the maximum value returned for a column. Applies to columns of type NUMBER, CHAR, VARCHAR2, NCHAR, and NVARCHAR2.

MIN[IMUM]

Computes the minimum value returned for a column. Applies to columns of type NUMBER, CHAR, VARCHAR2, NCHAR, and NVARCHAR2.

NUM[BER]

Performs a function similar to COUNT but computes the number of all values, including nulls.

STD

Computes the standard deviation of all non-null values for a numeric column.

SUM

Computes the sum of all non-null values for a numeric column.

VAR[IANCE]

Computes the variance of all non-null values for a numeric column.

LABEL

Allows you to specify a label for the computed value. If possible, this label will be printed to the left of the computed value.

label_text

Is the text you want to use as a label when the computed value is printed.

---

column_name

Is the name of the column you are summarizing. If it's a computed column, the expression is the name. If your SELECT statement aliases the column, you must use that alias name here.

group_column_name

Causes SQL*Plus to restart the calculation every time this column changes.

ROW

Causes the computation to be performed once for each row returned by the query.

REPORT

Causes the computation to be performed at the end of the report and to include values from all rows. REPORT is used for grand totals.

CONNECT

```
CONN[ECT] [username[/password][@connect] |
    / ] [AS {SYSOPER | SYSDBA}] | [INTERNAL]
```

The CONNECT command is used to change your database connection, log in as a different user, or connect to the database in an administrative mode. For example:

```
CONNECT SYSTEM/MANAGER@EMPDB
CONNECT /
CONNECT SYSTEM/MANAGER AS SYSDBA
```

Parameters

username

Is your database username.

password

Is your database password.

connect

Is the connect string or host string telling SQL*Plus the database to which you want to connect.

/   Allows you to use a forward slash instead of your user-name, password, and connect string when you want to connect to a local database using operating-system authentication.

AS

Tells SQL*Plus you are connecting in an administrative role.

SYSOPER

Tells SQL*Plus you are connecting as an operator.

SYSDBA

Tells SQL*Plus you are connecting as a database administrator.

INTERNAL

Tells SQL*Plus you want to connect internally.

COPY

```
COPY {FROM connection | TO connection}
     {APPEND | CREATE | INSERT | REPLACE}
     destination_table [(column_list)]
     USING select_statement
```

The COPY command allows you to use SQL*Plus as a conduit for transferring data between two Oracle databases. For example:

```
COPY FROM jeff/bigkid@empdb -
CREATE emp_names (id, name) -
USING SELECT employee_id, employee_name -
     FROM employee
```

Parameters

FROM/TO

Specifies either the target or the source database. You must be connected to one database. Use this clause to specify the other.

---

connection

Is the login information to use when connecting to the other database. This must be in the typical *username/ password@connect_string* format.

APP[END]

Causes SQL*Plus to insert the copied rows into the destination table. If necessary, SQL*Plus will create the destination table first.

CRE[ATE]

Causes SQL*Plus to copy the data only if the destination table is a new table.

INSERT

Causes SQL*Plus to insert the copied rows into the destination table only if it already exists.

REP[LACE]

Causes SQL*Plus to delete and recreate the destination table if it currently exists.

destination_table

Is the name of the table to which you want to copy the data.

column_list

Specifies column names to use when the COPY command creates a new destination table. This is a comma-delimited list, and the number of column names must match the number of columns in the SELECT statement.

select_statement

Is a SELECT statement that returns the data you want to COPY.

DEFINE

```
DEF[INE] [variable_name [= text]]
```

The DEFINE command allows you to create a user variable (or substitution variable) and to assign it a value. For example:

```
DEFINE company_name = "The Fictional Company"
```

You can also use DEFINE to list the value of one variable, or to list the values of all variables, as shown in these two examples:

```
DEFINE company_name
DEFINE
```

Parameters

variable_name

> Is the name of the variable you want to create. Issue the command with only a variable name, and SQL*Plus will display the current contents of that variable, if it exists.

text

> Is the text you want to assign to the variable.

DEL

```
DEL [{b | * | LAST}[ {e | * | LAST}]]
```

The DEL command is an editing command used to delete one or more lines from the buffer. For example:

```
DEL *
DEL 2 3
DEL 2 LAST
```

Parameters

b. Is a line number representing either a line to delete or the beginning of a range of lines to delete.

e. Is a line number representing the end of a range of lines to delete.

. Refers to the current line.

LAST

> Refers to the last line in the buffer.

DESCRIBE

```
DESC[RIBE] [schema.]object_name
           [@database_link_name]
```

The DESCRIBE command is used to display information about a table, a view, an Oracle8 object type, a stored package, a stored procedure, or a stored function. For example:

```
DESCRIBE employee
DESCRIBE jenny.employee
DESCRIBE employee@other_db
```

Parameters

schema
    Is the name of the object's owner.

object_name
    Is the name of the object that you want to describe.

database_link_name
    Is the name of a database link pointing to the database where the object exists.

DISCONNECT

```
DISC[ONNECT]
```

The DISCONNECT command closes your database connection without terminating SQL*Plus.

EDIT

```
ED[IT] [filename]
```

The EDIT command allows you to invoke an external editor to edit the contents of the SQL buffer or to edit the contents of an operating system file. For example:

```
EDIT
EDIT $ORACLE_BASE/admin/orcl/pfile/init.ora
```

The first command—with no parameter—allows you to edit the contents of the SQL buffer. The second allows you to edit a file.

EXECUTE

```
EXEC[UTE] statement
```

The EXECUTE command allows you to execute a single PL/SQL statement. For example:

```
EXECUTE DBMS_OUTPUT.PUT_LINE('Hi There');
```

The *statement* is the PL/SQL statement you want to execute.

EXIT

```
EXIT [SUCCESS | FAILURE | WARNING |
      value | user_variable | :bind_variable]
     [COMMIT | ROLLBACK]
```

The EXIT command is used to terminate a SQL*Plus session and return to the operating system. For example:

```
EXIT
EXIT SUCCESS
EXIT FAILURE ROLLBACK
```

Parameters

SUCCESS

  Returns a success status. This is the default.

FAILURE

  Returns a failure status.

WARNING

  Returns a warning status.

value

  Returns an arbitrary value as the status.

user_variable

Returns the value of the specified user variable as the status.

NOTE

SQL.SQLCODE is considered a user variable, as are all the other variables listed in Table 8.

:bind_variable

Returns the value of the specified bind variable as the status.

COMMIT

Causes SQL*Plus to commit before exiting. This is the default.

ROLLBACK

Causes SQL*Plus to roll back any open transaction before exiting.

GET

```
GET filename [LIS[T] | NOL[IST]]
```

The GET command reads a SQL statement from a file and loads it into the buffer. For example:

```
GET my_report.sql
GET my_report NOLIST
```

Parameters

filename

Is the name of the file containing the SQL statement you want to load.

LIST

Causes SQL*Plus to display the buffer after loading the file. This is the default.

NOL[IST]

Causes SQL*Plus to load the file without displaying it.

HELP

```
HELP [topic]
```

The HELP command is used to get help on SQL*Plus commands. Prior to the release of Oracle8*i* (8.1), HELP would also provide information on SQL and PL/SQL syntax. For example:

```
HELP MENU
HELP DESCRIBE
```

The *topic* is the help topic you want to read about. Entering HELP MENU will get you a complete list of valid topics.

NOTE

The Windows versions of SQL*Plus do not support on-line help.

HOST

```
HO[ST] [os_command]
```

The HOST command allows you to execute an operating-system command or invoke the command interpreter so that you can execute several such commands. Issuing HOST without specifying a command will get you a command prompt from which you may enter several commands.

The *os_command* is an operating-system command that you wish to execute.

INPUT

```
I[NPUT] [text]
```

Inserts one or more lines of text into the buffer. The lines are inserted after the current line. When you issue the

---

INSERT command with no text after it, SQL*Plus puts you
in insert mode, allowing you to type as many lines as you
like. Here's an example of INPUT being used:

```
SQL> L
  1   SELECT
  2*  FROM dual
SQL> L 1
  1*  SELECT
SQL> I *
SQL> L
  1   SELECT
  2   *
  3*  FROM dual
```

The *text* is the text you want to insert. Use this if you are
inserting only one line.

LIST

    L[IST] [{b | * | LAST}[{e | * | LAST}]]

The LIST command is an editing command used to list the
current line from the buffer. Issuing LIST by itself will
cause SQL*Plus to display all lines in the buffer. For
example:

```
SQL> L
  1   SELECT
  2   *
  3*  FROM dual
SQL> L 2 *
  2   *
  3*  FROM dual
SQL> L 1 LAST
  1   SELECT
  2   *
  3*  FROM dual
```

Parameters

b Is a line number representing the beginning of a range of lines to list. If no ending line number is specified, only this one line will be listed.

e Is a line number representing the end of a range of lines to list.

* Refers to the current line number.

LAST
    Refers to the last line in the buffer.

PASSWORD

```
PASSW[ORD] [username]
```

The PASSWORD command allows you to change your Oracle password using SQL*Plus. For example:

```
SQL> PASSWORD
Changing password for JONATHAN
Old password: ********
New password: ********
Retype new password: ********
Password changed
```

The *username* is the user whose password you want to change. The default is to change your own password. You need the ALTER USER privilege to change another user's password.

PAUSE

```
PAU[SE] [pause_message]
```

The PAUSE command is used to tell SQL*Plus to display a message and pause. The user must then press the ENTER key in order to continue. For example:

```
PAUSE "Press ENTER to continue."
```

The *pause_message* is an optional message that you want displayed to the user.

PRINT

```
PRI[NT] [bind_variable_name]
```

The PRINT command is used to display the value of a bind variable. For example:

```
PRINT x
```

The *bind_variable_name* is the name of the bind variable you want to print. If you omit a name, the values of all bind variables are printed.

PROMPT

```
PRO[MPT] text_to_be_displayed
```

The PROMPT command is used to display a message for the user to see.

The *text_to_be_displayed* is whatever text you want displayed to the user.

NOTE

The prompt string should not be quoted. If you include quotes, they will appear in the output.

QUIT

```
QUIT FAILURE ROLLBACK
    QUIT [SUCCESS | FAILURE | WARNING |
        value | user_variable |
          :bind_variable] |
        [COMMIT | ROLLBACK]
```

See EXIT for parameter descriptions. QUIT functions identically to EXIT.

RECOVER

```
RECOVER [DATABASE [[UNTIL
    {CANCEL
    | CHANGE system_change_number
    | TIME date_time}
    [USING BACKUP CONTROLFILE]
    [PARALLEL([DEGREE {num_of_procs | DEFAULT}
    | INSTANCES {num_of_inst | DEFAULT}]...)
    | NOPARALLEL] |

RECOVER TABLESPACE tablespace_name
    [,tablespace_name...]
    [PARALLEL([DEGREE {num_of_procs | DEFAULT}
    | INSTANCES {num_of_inst | DEFAULT}]...)
    | NOPARALLEL] |

RECOVER DATAFILE
    datafile_name [,datafile_name...]
    [PARALLEL([DEGREE {num_of_procs | DEFAULT}
    | INSTANCES {num_of_inst | DEFAULT}]...)
    | NOPARALLEL]
```

The RECOVER command initiates media recovery on a database, tablespace, or datafile. You must be connected as SYSDBA, SYSOPER, or INTERNAL in order to use RECOVER. Here are some examples:

```
RECOVER TABLESPACE users
RECOVER DATABASE UNTIL -
    TIME 20-JAN-2000:16:57:00
```

Parameters

RECOVER DATABASE

    Initiates media recovery on the entire database. The database must be mounted but not open.

RECOVER TABLESPACE *tablespace_name*

    Initiates media recovery on the specified tablespace or list of tablespaces (up to a maximum of 16). The tablespace(s) must be offline, and the database must be mounted and open.

RECOVER DATAFILE *datafile_name*

Initiates media recovery on the specified datafile or list of datafiles. The datafiles to be recovered must be offline. As long as none of the datafiles are part of the SYSTEM tablespace, the database may remain open.

UNTIL CANCEL

Allows you to recover one log file at a time, with the opportunity to cancel after each log file has been processed.

UNTIL CHANGE *system_change_number*

Performs an incomplete recovery based on the system change number. Note that the transaction with the specified number is not recovered.

UNTIL TIME *date_time*

Performs a time-based recovery. All transactions that were completed prior to the time specified are recovered.

USING BACKUP CONTROLFILE

Causes recovery to use a backup control file.

PARALLEL

Causes recovery to be done in parallel.

NOPARALLEL

Prevents recovery from being done in parallel.

DEGREE {*num_of_procs* | DEFAULT}

Controls the number of recovery processes running in parallel for each instance. You may specify a number or use the DEFAULT keyword. DEFAULT causes the number of processes to equal twice the number of datafiles being recovered.

INSTANCES {*num_of_procs* | DEFAULT}

Controls the number of instances that may be used in a parallel recovery. You may specify a number or use the

DEFAULT keyword. The number of instances used when DEFAULT is specified is operating-system specific.

REMARK

```
REM[ARK] comment_text
```

The REMARK command is used to place comments in a SQL*Plus script. For example:

```
REM This script written by Justin Nue.
```

The *comment_text* is your comment.

REPFOOTER

```
REPF[OOTER] [OFF | ON] |
    [COL x | S[KIP] x | TAB x | LE[FT] |
        CE[NTER] | R[IGHT] | BOLD |
        FOR[MAT] format_spec | text |
            variable...]
```

The REPFOOTER command defines a report footer. Report footers print on the last page of a report—after the last detail line and before the bottom title. See REPHEADER for parameter descriptions.

REPHEADER

```
REPH[EADER] [OFF | ON] |
    [COL x | S[KIP] x | TAB x | LE[FT] |
    CE[NTER] | R[IGHT] | BOLD | FOR[MAT]
    format_spec | text | variable...]
```

The REPHEADER command defines a report header. Report headers print on the first page of a report—after the page title and before the first detail line. See TTITLE for parameter descriptions.

RUN

```
R[UN]
```

The RUN command displays and then executes the command currently in the SQL buffer. For example:

```
SQL> R
  1* SELECT USER FROM dual

USER
- - - - - - - - - - - - - - - - - - - - - - - - - - - - -
JONATHAN
```

SAVE

```
SAV[E] filename [CRE[ATE] | REP[LACE] |
    APP[END]]
```

The SAVE command writes the contents of the SQL buffer to an operating-system file. For example:

```
SAVE my_query.sql
SAVE my_query REPLACE
```

Parameters

filename

Is the name of the file to which you want to write the buffer contents.

CRE[ATE]

Causes the operation to succeed only if the file does not already exist. This is the default.

REP[LACE]

Overwrites any existing file of the same name.

APP[END]

Appends the contents of the buffer to the file.

SET

```
SET parameter_setting
```

The SET command is used to customize SQL*Plus' operations to your needs. For example:

```
SET DEFINE OFF
SET SERVEROUTPUT ON SIZE 1000000 -
    FORMAT WORD_WRAPPED
SET NULL '***'
```

Parameter Settings

SET APPI[NFO] {ON | OFF | *app_text*}

Controls automatic registration of command files using the DBMS_APPLICATION_INFO package.

SET ARRAY[SIZE] *array_size*

Sets the number of rows that SQL*Plus will return at one time from the database when executing a query. The default is 1.

SET AUTO[COMMIT] {ON | OFF | IMMEDIATE | *statement_count*}

Controls whether SQL*Plus automatically commits your changes. Also specifies the number of statements to allow between each commit.

SET AUTOP[RINT] {ON | OFF}

Controls whether SQL*Plus automatically prints the contents of bind variables after they have been referenced in a SQL statement or PL/SQL block.

SET AUTORECOVERY {ON | OFF}

When turned on, allows the RECOVER command to run without user intervention.

SET AUTOT[RACE] {ON | OFF | TRACE[ONLY]} [EXP[LAIN]] [STAT[ISTICS]]

Enables and disables the automatic display of the execution plan and execution statistics for a SQL statement.

SET BLO[CKTERMINATOR] *block_term_char*

Sets the character used to terminate entry of a PL/SQL block. The default is a period.

SET BUF[FER] {*buffer_name* | SQL}

Allows you to switch between buffers. Note that only one buffer can be used for executing SQL statements.

SET CLOSECUR[SOR] {ON | OFF}

Controls whether SQL*Plus keeps the statement cursor open all the time.

SET CMDS[EP] {ON | OFF | *separator_char*}

Controls whether you can enter multiple SQL statements on one line and also sets the separator character. If you turn this option on, then the default separator character is a semicolon.

SET COLSEP *column_separator*

Controls the text used to separate columns of data. The default is to separate columns using one space.

SET COM[PATIBILITY] {V7 | V8 | NATIVE}

Specifies the Oracle release with which SQL*Plus should be compatible. The default behavior is to let SQL*Plus decide this automatically.

SET CON[CAT] {ON | OFF | *concat_char*}

Specifies the concatenation character, which marks the end of a substitution variable name in a SQL*Plus statement, SQL statement, or PL/SQL block. The default character is a period.

SET COPYC[OMMIT] *batch_count*

Controls how often SQL*Plus commits during the execution of a COPY command. The default is 0.

SET COPYTYPECHECK {ON | OFF}

Controls whether type checking is done when using the COPY command to copy data from one table to another.

SET DEF[INE] {ON | OFF | *prefix_char*}

Specifies the character used to define a substitution variable. The default is the ampersand character (&).

SET DOC[UMENT] {<u>ON</u> | OFF}

Controls whether SQL*Plus displays documentation demarcated by the DOCUMENT command.

SET ECHO {ON | <u>OFF</u>}

Controls whether SQL*Plus displays commands from a command file as they are executed.

SET EDITF[ILE] *edit_filename*

Specifies the name of the work file used when you invoke an external editor using the EDIT command. The default name is *afiedt.buf.*

SET EMB[EDDED] {ON | <u>OFF</u>}

Enables and disables the embedded report feature. This allows you to combine two reports into one without resetting the page numbering.

SET ESC[APE] {ON | <u>OFF</u> | *escape_char*}

Specifies the escape character, which is used in front of the substitution variable prefix character (usually an ampersand), when you want that character interpreted literally and not as part of a variable name. The default character is a backslash (\).

SET FEED[BACK] {<u>ON</u> | OFF | *row_threshold*}

Controls whether and when SQL*Plus displays the number of rows affected by a SQL statement.

SET FLAGGER {<u>OFF</u> | ENTRY | INTERMED[IATE] | FULL}

Controls whether SQL*Plus checks your statements for compliance with ANSI/ISO syntax.

SET FLU[SH] {<u>ON</u> | OFF}

Controls whether output may be buffered.

SET HEA[DING] [<u>ON</u> | OFF]

Controls whether column headings are displayed when selecting data.

SET HEADS[EP] {<u>ON</u> | OFF | *heading_separator*}

Controls the character used to make a line break in a column heading. The default is a vertical bar (|).

SET INSTANCE [*service_name* | LOCAL]

Specifies the default database instance to use with the CONNECT command.

SET LIN[ESIZE] *line_width*

Specifies the size of a line in terms of characters. The default LINESIZE is 80 characters.

SET LOBOF[FSET] *offset*

Is an index into a LONG column, specifying the first character to be displayed. The default is 1.

SET LOGSOURCE *logpath*

Tells SQL*Plus where to find archive log files for recovery. There is no default.

SET LONG *long_length*

Specifies the maximum number of characters to display from a column of type LONG. The default is 80.

SET LONGC[HUNKSIZE] *size*

Controls the number of characters retrieved from a LONG column at one time. The default is 80.

SET MAXD[ATA] *max_row_width*

Sets the maximum row length that SQL*Plus can handle. This is an obsolete setting, and there is no default.

SET MARK[UP] *markup_options*

Allows you to specify the markup language to use when generating output. Except for HTML, all markup options are optional. The following are valid markup options:

HTML [ON | OFF]

Specifies the markup language to use and enables or disables the use of that markup language. In release 8.1.6, this is a mandatory option.

HEAD *text*

Specifies content for the <head> tag. The tag ends up being written as <head *text*>. There is no default.

BODY *text*

    Specifies content for the \<body\> tag. The tag ends up being written as \<body *text*\>. There is no default.

ENTMAP {<u>ON</u> | OFF}

    Controls whether SQL*Plus uses HTML equivalents such as < and > for special characters.

SPOOL {ON | <u>OFF</u>}

    Controls whether SQL*Plus writes to the spool file using plain text or the specified markup language (currently HTML).

PRE[FORMAT] {ON | <u>OFF</u>}

    Controls whether spooled report output is enclosed within \<pre\>...\</pre\> tags.

On some operating systems, you need to enclose the entire string of markup options within double quotes.

SET NEWP[AGE] {*lines_to_print* | NONE}

Controls the number of lines that SQL*Plus prints between pages. A value of zero causes SQL*Plus to print a form-feed character between each page. The default is 1.

SET NULL *null_text*

Controls the text that SQL*Plus uses to represent a null value. The default is to represent nulls by a space.

SET NUMF[ORMAT] *format_spec*

Sets the default display format for numbers. There is no default format.

SET NUM[WIDTH] *width*

Sets the default display width for numbers. SET NUM-FORMAT takes precedence over this value. The default width is 9.

SET PAGES[IZE] *lines_on_page*

Specifies the number of printable lines on a page. The default is 24.

SET PAU[SE] {ON | <u>OFF</u> | *pause_message*}

Controls whether SQL*Plus pauses after each page of output.

SET RECSEP {<u>WR[APPED]</u> | EA[CH] | OFF}

Controls whether a record-separator line is printed between lines of output. The default is to print separators only when one of the column values in a record has wrapped.

SET RECSEPCHAR *separator_char*

Controls the character to use for the record separator. The default record separator is a line of space characters.

SET SCAN {<u>ON</u> | OFF}

Enables and disables user variable substitution. This is obsolete in favor of SET DEFINE.

SET SERVEROUT[PUT] {ON | <u>OFF</u>}
[SIZE *buffer_size*] [FOR[MAT] {WRA[PPED] |
<u>WOR[D_WRAPPED]</u> | TRU[NCATED]}]

Controls whether SQL*Plus prints output from PL/SQL blocks.

SET SHIFT[INOUT] {VIS[IBLE] | <u>INV[ISIBLE]</u>}

Controls the display of shift characters on IBM 3270 terminals.

SET SHOW[MODE] {ON | <u>OFF</u> | BOTH}

Controls whether SQL*Plus displays the before and after values when you change a setting.

SET SPACE *num_of_spaces*

Specifies the number of spaces to print between columns. The default is 1. This is obsolete in favor of SET COLSEP.

SET SQLBLANKLINES {ON | <u>OFF</u>}

Controls whether you may enter blank lines as part of a SQL statement. This feature was introduced in release 8.1.5.

SET SQLC[ASE] {MIXED | UPPER | LOWER}
Controls automatic case conversion of SQL statements and PL/SQL blocks.

SET SQLCO[NTINUE] *continuation_prompt*
Allows you to change the continuation prompt used for multiline SQL statements. The default is greater-than (>).

SET SQLN[UMBER] {ON | OFF}
Controls whether SQL*Plus uses the line number as a prompt when you enter a multiline SQL statement.

SET SQLPRE[FIX] *prefix_char*
Specifies the SQL*Plus prefix character, which allows you to execute a SQL*Plus command while entering a SQL statement or PL/SQL block into the buffer. The default is a pound sign (#).

SET SQLP[ROMPT] *prompt_text*
Allows you to change the SQL*Plus command prompt. The default is SQL>.

SET SQLT[ERMINATOR] {ON | OFF | *term_char*}
Controls whether terminating a SQL statement using the semicolon causes it to be executed. Also allows you to change the termination character to something other than a semicolon.

SET SUF[FIX] *extension*
Specifies the default extension used for command files. The default is *.sql*.

SET TAB {ON | OFF}
Controls whether SQL*Plus uses tab characters to format whitespace.

SET TERM[OUT] {ON | OFF}
Controls whether SQL*Plus displays output generated from a SQL*Plus script file.

SET TI[ME] {ON | OFF}
Controls whether SQL*Plus displays the current time as part of the command prompt.

SET TIMI[NG] {ON | <u>OFF</u>}
    Controls whether SQL*Plus displays the elapsed execution time for each SQL statement or PL/SQL block.

SET TRIM[OUT] {<u>ON</u> | OFF}
    Controls whether SQL*Plus trims trailing spaces from lines displayed on the screen.

SET TRIMS[POOL] {ON | <u>OFF</u>}
    Controls whether SQL*Plus trims trailing spaces from lines written to a spool file.

SET TRU[NCATE] {ON | <u>OFF</u>}
    Controls whether SQL*Plus truncates long lines.

SET UND[ERLINE] {*underline_char* | {<u>ON</u> | OFF}}
    Sets the character used to underline column headings. The default is a hyphen.

SET VER[IFY] {<u>ON</u> | OFF}
    Controls whether SQL*Plus displays before and after images of lines containing substitution variables.

SET WRA[P] {<u>ON</u> | OFF}
    Controls whether SQL*Plus wraps or truncates long lines.

SHOW

```
SHO[W] [ | setting |
    ALL | BTI[TLE] |
    ERR[ORS] [{FUNCTION | PROCEDURE | PACKAGE |
              PACKAGE BODY | TRIGGER | TYPE |
              TYPE BODY | VIEW}
              [owner.]object_name] |
    LNO | PARAMETER[S] [parameter_name] |
    PNO | REL[EASE] | REPF[OOTER] |
        REPH[EADER] |
    SGA | SPOO[L] | SQLCODE | TTI[TLE] |
        USER]
```

The SHOW command allows you to look at the current state of your SQL*Plus environment. For example:

```
SHOW PARAMETER db_block_buffers
SHOW LINESIZE
SHOW TTITLE
```

Parameters

setting

Is any one of the settings you can set using the SET command.

ALL

Shows everything, except for errors and the System Global Area (SGA).

BTI[TLE]

Displays the current page footer.

ERR[ORS]

Displays an error listing for a stored object. The command SHOW ERRORS by itself causes the error listing for the most recently created object to be displayed. You can get the error listing for a specific object by specifying the object type (function, procedure, and so forth) and the object name.

FUNCTION | PROCEDURE | PACKAGE | PACKAGE BODY | TRIGGER | TYPE | TYPE BODY | VIEW

Used with SHOW ERRORS to specify the object type of interest.

[*owner.*]*object_name*

Used with SHOW ERRORS to name the object for which you want to display an error listing.

LNO

Displays the current line number.

PARAMETER[S] [*parameter_name*]

Displays the current value of one or more database initialization parameters.

PNO

Displays the current page number.

REL[EASE]

Displays the release number (the version) of the Oracle database to which you are connected.

REPF[OOTER]

Displays the current report footer.

REPH[EADER]

Displays the current report header.

SGA

Displays information about the current state of the System Global Area.

SPOO[L]

Tells you whether output is currently being spooled to a file.

SQLCODE

Displays the SQL code returned by the most recent SQL statement.

TTI[TLE]

Displays the current page title.

USER

Displays the current username.

SHUTDOWN

```
SHUTDOWN
    [NORMAL | IMMEDIATE | TRANSACTIONAL | ABORT]
```

The SHUTDOWN command allows you to stop an Oracle instance. In order to use SHUTDOWN, you must be connected as SYSDBA, SYSOPER, or INTERNAL. For example:

```
SHUTDOWN
SHUTDOWN IMMEDIATE
```

Parameters

NORMAL

> Oracle waits for all users to voluntarily disconnect before shutting down the instance. This is the default.

IMMEDIATE

> Oracle summarily disconnects each user as soon as his current SQL statement completes. Open transactions are rolled back.

TRANSACTIONAL

> Oracle waits for each user to complete his current transaction and then disconnects him.

ABORT

> All background processes for the instance are immediately aborted. Crash recovery will occur the next time the database is open, or if Oracle Parallel Server is being used, one of the surviving instances will recover the one that was aborted.

SPOOL

```
SP[OOL] filename | OFF | OUT
```

The SPOOL command causes output to be written to a text file. For example:

```
SPOOL c:\data\emp_pay_report
SPOOL OFF
```

Parameters

filename

> Is the name of the file to which you want to write the output. The default extension depends on the operating system and will be either LST or LIS. Under Windows 95 and NT, it is LST. A path may be specified as part of the filename.

OFF

Turns spooling off.

OUT

Turns spooling off and prints the file on the default printer. This option is not available in the Windows versions of SQL*Plus.

START

```
STA[RT] script_file [argument...]
```

START executes a SQL*Plus script. See @ for parameter descriptions. START and @ function identically.

STARTUP

```
STARTUP [FORCE] [RESTRICT]
        [PFILE = parameter_filename]
        [MOUNT [OPEN [RECOVER]]
        [database_name]]
        [[EXCLUSIVE | PARALLEL | SHARED]
        [RETRY]] | [NOMOUNT]
```

The STARTUP command allows you to start an Oracle instance and open a database. For example:

```
STARTUP
STARTUP RESTRICT
STARTUP PFILE = c:\temp\tempinit.ora
```

To use STARTUP, you must be connected as SYSDBA, SYSOPER, or INTERNAL.

Parameters

FORCE

Forces the instance to start. If the instance is currently running, then FORCE will cause the equivalent of a SHUTDOWN ABORT to be done first; the instance will then be restarted.

RESTRICT
    Opens the database in restricted session mode.

PFILE = *parameter_filename*
    Tells SQL*Plus to use the specified parameter file (initialization file) when starting the instance. You may specify a path with the filename.

NOTE

SQL*Plus reads the parameter file, not the Oracle instance. The path to the parameter file must be relative to the machine running SQL*Plus.

MOUNT
    Causes the database to be mounted but not opened.

OPEN
    Causes the database to be mounted and then opened for normal operation.

RECOVER
    Tells Oracle to perform media recovery, if necessary, before opening the database.

database_name
    Overrides the DB_NAME parameter in the initialization file.

EXCLUSIVE
    Causes the database to be opened or mounted exclusively by the current instance. No other instances may share it. This is the default setting and is used if neither SHARE nor PARALLEL is specified.

PARALLEL
    Causes the database to be opened or mounted so as to allow multiple instances to access it simultaneously.

SHARED
    Has the same effect as PARALLEL.

STORE

RETRY

Specifies the number of retry attempts when you open a database in parallel mode. Retries are five seconds apart.

NOMOUNT

Causes an instance to be started, but no database is mounted or opened.

STORE

```
STORE SET filename
    [CRE[ATE] | REP[LACE] | APP[END]]
```

STORE generates a file of SET commands based on the current state of those settings. For example:

```
STORE SET current_settings REPLACE
...
@current_settings
```

In this example, the first command stores the current settings while the second command restores those settings by executing the file generated by the STORE command.

Parameters

filename

Is the name of the file to which you want to write the SET commands.

CRE[ATE]

Causes the command to fail if the file already exists. This is the default.

REP[LACE]

Causes SQL*Plus to overwrite any existing file with the same name.

APP[END]

Appends the SET commands to an existing file.

TIMING

```
TIMI[NG] [START [timer_name] | SHOW | STOP]
```

The TIMING command lets you start, stop, or display the value of a timer in order to measure elapsed time. For example:

```
TIMING START emp_query_timer
TIMING SHOW
TIMING STOP
```

Parameters

START [*timer_name*]

Starts a new timer and optionally gives it the name you provide.

SHOW

Shows the current value of the most recently started timer.

STOP

Stops the most recently started timer, shows its current value, and then deletes it.

TTITLE

```
TTI[TLE] [OFF | ON] |
    [COL x | S[KIP] x | TAB x | LE[FT] |
    CE[NTER] | R[IGHT] | BOLD | FOR[MAT]
    format_spec | text | variable...]
```

The TTITLE command defines page titles for a report. For example:

```
TTITLE CENTER 'The Fictional Company' SKIP 3 -
LEFT 'I.S. Department' -
RIGHT 'Project Hours and Dollars Report'
TITLE RIGHT FORMAT 999 SQL.PNO
```

Issuing the TTITLE command with no parameters causes SQL*Plus to display the current setting.

Parameters

OFF

Turns off the page title but does not erase its definition.

ON

Turns on the printing of page titles.

COL *x*

Causes any title text following this parameter to print at the specified column position.

S[KIP] *x*

Inserts the specified number of line breaks before printing any subsequent title text.

TAB *x*

Skips forward the specified number of character columns. Negative values cause SQL*Plus to skip backwards.

LE[FT]

Causes subsequent title text to be printed beginning at the leftmost column of the current title line.

CE[NTER]

Causes subsequent title text to be centered within the current line.

R[IGHT]

Causes subsequent title text to be printed flush right.

BOLD

Makes your title bold by printing it three times. Only title text following the BOLD command is repeated on each line.

FOR[MAT]

Allows you to control how subsequent numeric data in the title is displayed.

format_spec

Is a string that specifies the display format to use for subsequent numeric data in the title.

text

    Is any text you want to have in the title.

variable

    Inserts the value of the specified user variable. You may also use one of the system variables maintained by SQL*Plus. These are described in Table 8.

*Table 8. SQL*Plus System Variables*

System Variable	Value
SQL.PNO	The current page number.
SQL.LNO	The current line number.
SQL.RELEASE	The current Oracle release.
SQL.SQLCODE	The error code returned by the most recent SQL query.
SQL.USER	The Oracle username of the user running the report.

UNDEFINE

```
UNDEF[INE] variable_name [variable_name...]
```

The UNDEFINE command erases a user variable definition. For example:

```
UNDEFINE emp_name
UNDEFINE emp_name proj_name
```

The *variable_name* is the name of a user variable to delete. You can delete several variables with one command by listing them separated by spaces.

VARIABLE

```
VAR[IABLE] [variable_name [data_type]]
```

The VARIABLE command is used to declare bind variables. For example:

```
VARIABLE x NUMBER
VARIABLE query_results REFCURSOR
VARIABLE emp_name VARCHAR2(40)
```

Bind variables are real variables that can be used within a PL/SQL block or SQL statement. Issuing the VARIABLE command with no parameters generates a list of all currently defined bind variables.

Parameters

variable_name

Is the name you want to give the variable. If you stop here and don't supply a datatype, SQL*Plus displays the datatype for the variable that you have named.

data_type

Is the datatype of the variable. The following datatypes are allowed:

NUMBER

Results in a floating-point number and is the same as a NUMBER variable in PL/SQL or a NUMBER column in a table. Unlike PL/SQL, SQL*Plus does not let you specify a length or a precision, so a declaration like NUMBER (9,2) is not allowed.

CHAR [(*length*)]

Results in a fixed-length character string. Length is optional. If it's omitted, you get a one-character string.

NCHAR [(*length*)]

Results in a fixed-length character string in the national character set. Length is optional. If it's omitted, you get a one-character string.

VARCHAR2 (*length*)

Results in a variable-length character string.

NVARCHAR2 (*length*)

Results in a variable-length character string using the national language character set.

CLOB

Results in a character large object variable.

NCLOB

Results in a character large object variable using the national language character set.

REFCURSOR

Gives you a cursor variable you can use to return the results of a SQL query from PL/SQL to SQL*Plus.

WHENEVER

```
WHENEVER {OSERROR | SQLERROR}
    {EXIT [SUCCESS | FAILURE |
        value | :bind_variable |]
          [COMMIT | ROLLBACK] |
    CONTINUE [COMMIT | ROLLBACK | NONE]}
```

The WHENEVER command controls the behavior of SQL*Plus when an operating-system error or a SQL error occurs. For example:

```
WHENEVER OSERROR EXIT FAILURE
WHENEVER SQLERROR EXIT FAILURE ROLLBACK
```

Parameters

WHENEVER OSERROR

Use this form of the command to tell SQL*Plus what to do in the event of an operating-system error.

WHENEVER SQLERROR

Use this form of the command to tell SQL*Plus what to do when an error is returned from a SQL statement or a PL/SQL block.

EXIT SUCCESS
> Exit with a success status.

EXIT FAILURE
> Exit with a failure status.

EXIT *value*
> Exit and return the value specified as the status. The value may be a literal or a user variable.

EXIT *:bind_variable*
> Exit and return the value of the specified bind variable as the status.

CONTINUE
> Do not exit if an error occurs. This is the default behavior when you first start SQL*Plus.

COMMIT
> May be used in conjunction with both EXIT and CONTINUE. It causes SQL*Plus to COMMIT the current transaction when an error occurs. This is the default behavior when you use the EXIT keyword.

ROLLBACK
> May be used in conjunction with EXIT and CONTINUE and causes SQL*Plus to roll back the current transaction when an error occurs.

NONE
> May only be used in conjunction with CONTINUE and causes SQL*Plus to neither COMMIT nor ROLLBACK when an error occurs. This is the default behavior when you use the CONTINUE keyword.

Oracle

Oracle Built-in Packages

By Steven Feuerstein, Charles Dye & John Beresniewicz
1st Edition April 1998
956 pages, Includes diskette
ISBN 1-56592-375-8

Oracle's built-in packages dramatically extend the power of the PL/SQL language, but few developers know how to use them effectively. This book is a complete reference to all of the built-ins, including those new to Oracle8. The enclosed diskette includes an online tool that provides easy access to the many files of source code and documentation developed by the authors.

Oracle SQL*Plus: The Definitive Guide

By Jonathan Gennick
1st Edition March 1999
526 pages, ISBN 1-56592-578-5

This book is the definitive guide to SQL*Plus, Oracle's interactive query tool. Despite the wide availability and usage of SQL*Plus, few developers and DBAs know how powerful it really is. This book introduces SQL*Plus, provides a syntax quick reference, and describes how to write and execute script files, generate ad hoc reports, extract data from the database, query the data dictionary tables, use the SQL*Plus administrative features (new in Oracle8i), and much more.

Oracle Web Applications: PL/SQL Developer's Introduction

By Andrew Odewahn
1st Edition September 1999
256 pages, ISBN 1-56592-687-0

This book is an easy-to-understand guide to building Oracle8i (Oracle's "Internet database") Web applications using a variety of tools – PL/SQL, HTML, XML, WebDB, and Oracle Application Server (OAS). It also covers the packages in the PL/SQL toolkit and demonstrates several fully realized Web applications. This book provides the jump-start you need to extend relational concepts to Web content and to make the transition from traditional programming to the development of useful Web applications for Oracle8i. Also covers Web development for Oracle8 and Oracle7.

O'REILLY®